Conversation Skills

On the Job and in the Community

A Curriculum for Adolescents and Adults With Developmental Disabilities

Marilyn Banks, Ed.D.

IEP

RESOURCES

Win/Mac CD

This CD contains a printable PDF of the entire book. You can review and print pages from your computer. The PDF (portable document format) file requires **Acrobat Reader** software.

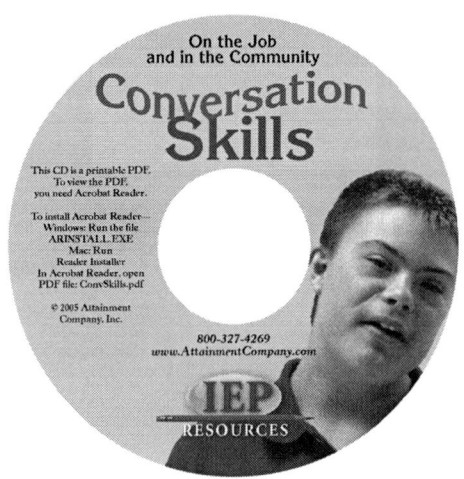

- If you have **Acrobat Reader** already on your computer, run the program and then open the file using **ConvSkills.pdf** from the CD.

- **To Install Acrobat Reader for Windows**: Run **ARINSTALL.EXE** provided on the CD. After installation, run Acrobat Reader then open using **ConvSkills.pdf**

- **To install Acrobat Reader for Mac**: Run **Reader Installer**. After installation, open using **ConvSkills.pdf**

Author: Marilyn Banks, Ed.D.
Editor: Tom Kinney
Graphic Design: Sherry Pribbenow

An Attainment Publication

ISBN 1-575861-545-3

RESOURCES

Attainment Company

P.O. Box 930160
Verona, Wisconsin 53593-0160
Phone 800-327-4269   Fax 800.942.3865
www.AttainmentCompany.com

Table of Contents

Appendix   91

About the Author

Dr. Marilyn Banks, Ed.D.

Dr. Banks received her Bachelor of Science degree in Speech and Language Pathology at Kent State University, her Masters of Science in Interrelated Special Education from Georgia State University, and her Doctorate in Child and Youth Studies from Nova Southeastern University. She also holds teaching certificates in Behavior Disorders and Mental Retardation.

Her career has been enriched by serving as an elementary school Speech and Language Pathologist, the teaching of reading in a private school, a high school resource teacher for Behavior Disorders/Learning Disabilities, and a high school Vocational Instructor for students with Developmental Disabilities. She is presently employed as a Vocational Instructor for high school students in the Cobb County Public Schools in Marietta, Georgia. In her present position, Dr. Banks coordinates vocational assessment labs for students with Mild Intellectual Disabilities in 14 high schools in her county, and interacts with local businesses to train students in work related behaviors.

Dr. Banks has written classroom curriculum for students with emotional disabilities and transition curriculum for students with severe developmental disabilities. She is a member of the American Association for Mental Retardation and the Council for Exceptional Children. She authored the Eagle Project as a result of years of observing workers with disabilities function as loners during non-work periods.

She resides in Marietta, Georgia with her husband, Lucas and her 17-year-old daughter, Katie.

Introduction
Learning Interactive Conversation Skills

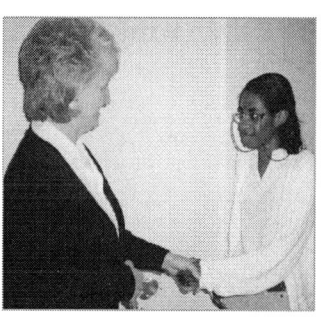

Originally titled the Eagle Project for Conversation Interaction Skills, this program is an exciting self-paced method for teaching proactive talk. It was named Eagle Project because it turns its participants into high-soaring, independent leaders in the art of conversation. These 50-plus self-managed lessons constitute a course that has consistently amazed teachers and parents with positive results after only 12 weeks of training. In a world where etiquette, warmth and friendliness are on the wane, this course sets a new standard for initiating appropriate greetings, questions, and comments. When adult vocational instructors viewed videotapes of our field-testing, they remarked, "this kind of training would be helpful for everyone!"

While proactive social skills are necessary for all of us, they are particularly vital for people with cognitive disabilities. In addition, during an era in which the practice of traditional social skills has fallen on hard times, for students with disabilities to achieve a basic mastery of these skills gives them a leg up in the real world. Employers and others who will work with and relate to your students after high school will be positively impressed with them and are likely to go out of their way to help them succeed. There may be no better skill area to work on with your students than the **Conversation Skills** taught in this book.

These user-friendly lessons are designed to be implemented by classroom teachers, speech and language pathologists and vocational instructors. Students of varying abilities can learn to break the ice with engaging greetings and appropriate questions on a day-to-day basis. The simple-to-use sheets promote social integration and help students to make new acquaintances and lasting friendships.

Instructors need only to spend as little as 10 minutes twice weekly to teach these invaluable speaking skills. Participants role-play with the teacher, each other, and high profile peers in order to master simple phraseology that makes them the principle initiator of conversations. Students simply mark their self-managed sheets and report back to the classroom group weekly. Reinforcement is given through periodic reviews, certificates of achievement, and structured group commendation. In a short period of time, even nonreaders can use the meaningful graphics to remember techniques that enable them to socialize with peers, coworkers and neighbors. **Communication Skills** repertoires have been mastered by people of all abilities and are especially effective for those who have severe, moderate and mild developmental disabilities. The course is designed to help students practice skills across the environment and has been proven to provide a lasting bank of social tools for their future.

Instructors need only to spend as little as 10 minutes twice weekly to promote social integration and help students to make new acquaintances and lasting friendships.

Conversation Skills helps you answer the following questions and accomplish the following goals:

Why do students need social skills on the job?

Studies have repeatedly shown that young people with mild and moderate developmental disabilities do not initiate conversations and frequently exhibit behaviors that isolate them on the job. These young workers with developmental disabilities are often not fully integrated with other workers with whom they coexist. They often remain passive in conversations and forget to initiate greetings, comments or questions.

Notably, it has been pointed out that while most workers without disabilities lose their jobs for reasons of character, people with disabilities lose their jobs for social reasons. One of the goals of this program is to give a social booster shot to your students to immunize them against this outcome.

What skill sets does Conversation Skills teach and how?

Through guided practice and repetition, it provides young people with disabilities with a whole new set of social-communicative skills—50 plus in all—which are generalized across all relevant environments through use of self-managed checklists that are an integral part of **Conversation Skills**. The practice of, and repetition on, each skill is delivered in the 50 Lesson Objectives while generalization of each skill is held accountable through the 50 Self-Managed Checklists on the back side of the Lesson Objectives. Note that Self-Managed Checklists are picture-cued for nonreaders and each skill has its own icon. Discuss this with students.

How does Conversation Skills training work?

Teachers need only to spend as little as 10 minutes, twice weekly, in teaching students the most vital social conversation skills for a work environment. Virtually all lessons include suggested student role-plays with the teacher and each other in order to learn simple phraseology that allows them to be the initiator of conversations and provides them with a repertoire of conversation. Repeat these role-plays to the point of memorization. Periodic but simple Review Sheets reinforce learning and students are rewarded with Certificates of Accomplishment, included as reproducibles periodically throughout the book.

Who should participate in Conversation Skills training?

Students who need these 50 conversation skills. Using this program, essential, basic repertoires have been mastered by students with severe, moderate and mild developmental disabilities and they are the target users.

Each of the 50 **Conversation Skills** includes a Lesson page with a primary objective, a Self-Managed Checklist for the student on its reverse side, an occasional Review Sheet and periodic Certificates of Achievement.

Students role-play with the teacher and each other in order to learn simple phraseology that makes them the initiator of conversations and provides them with a repertoire of conversation.

Each lesson follows this structure:

Rationale:

The reason why students need to know this skill.

Objective:

Their goal in learning it.

Methods:

How you teach it.

Extra practice:

Additional helpful exercises.

Assignment Sheet:

Homework to help secure student acquisition of the skill.

Debriefing Session:

A reinforcing session to confirm that students have done their homework assignments and a review of the previous week's lesson.

Self-Managed Checklist

Found on the following page. Checklists help students to chart their success and progress with the skill of the week. Directions are at the top of each page and are self-explanatory.

Tinted areas indicate where the coworker or others should circle yes or no.

Time Allotted: 20 minutes

Lesson 2 Objective
Learn the Names of Your Coworkers & Friends

Week 1 — Day One

Rationale:
Too often young people with disabilities neglect to find out the names of coworkers, schoolmates or community contacts. They need to learn the skill of being the first to introduce themselves.

Objective:
Students will build on lesson one by having a brief review of their skill sheets. Ask students how they introduced themselves. Clap for all students, even shy ones who might not have taken any opportunities to introduce themselves. This is important because they will come around after seeing others take the plunge. Students will now begin to find out names of people of coworkers, schoolmates, administrators and neighbors.

Methods:
Have students practice by introducing themselves to each other, saying their own first and last names and asking the other person's name. Make sure each person acts as the initiator at least once. They say, "Hello, my name is _____, what is your name?"

Extra Practice:
If time permits, have several high profile peers from a class nearby come in and allow students to practice. Students might also go to the administration office and practice the introduction and name gathering.

Assignment Sheet:
After role-playing, teacher passes out assignment sheet #2. Students are instructed to write their names and the date on the sheet. This is important because if sheets get dropped or lost, they can be returned to the individual. Explain the sheet to the group and have them mark the first line with the name of the person they either met in class, in another class or in the building. This exercise is even good for adult learners because many of us might not know the names of all the people we come in contact with daily. After all, what is the sweetest sound in the human language? Isn't it our own name being used or called by someone? Remind students to use their own first and last names when they introduce themselves.

Week 3 — Day One

Debriefing Session:
Students have had two weeks of social interaction. They should be excited by now. Keep the momentum high now by offering small rewards for those who return sheets and have something written on them. Please refrain from scolding or taking anything away from those who are not in the groove yet. They will come around when they see others being commended and being successful! The whole group claps for everyone because these exercises are strictly voluntary and there is no right or wrong involved in this. Each person establishes his/her own norms. Encourage students to keep up the introductions as they meet new people. **Remember they are trying to be the initiator in all exercises.**

Lessons 5

Self-Managed Checklist

Lesson 20

Be the First to Ask Two Expansion Questions:

"Do You Have Any Pets?"

"How Many Pets do You Have?"

Student Name _____ Date _____

Be the first to ask your coworkers and friends if they have any pets and how many pets they have. After you ask the questions, circle a number and have the person write whether you were the first to ask the questions.

Do You Have Any Pets?

1 2 3 4 5

How Many Pets Do You Have?

1 2 3 4 5

1. Was the student the first to ask you the questions?	Yes	No
2. Was the student the first to ask you the questions?	Yes	No
3. Was the student the first to ask you the questions?	Yes	No

Main Features of Conversation Skills

- 50-plus self-managed lessons

- Covers the gamut of basic, necessary proactive conversation skills for a successful and fulfilling life in the community and at work

- Takes only 12 weeks of twice-weekly 10 minute training sessions

- Self-paced

- Involves hands-on role plays with staff and high-profile peers

- Students self-manage their accountability

Reasons These Skills are Vital for Students

- People with disabilities often fail to initiate conversations on the job, thereby isolating themselves

- Often those with developmental disabilities lose jobs because of social isolation, while nondisabled workers typically lose jobs because of character issues

- **Conversation Skills** gives students a ready and built-in social repertoire

Lessons

Lesson 1 Objective
Introduce Yourself

Week 1 — Day One

Rationale:

Young people with disabilities do not always take the initiative to introduce themselves when they meet new people.

Objective:

This lesson encourages students to introduce themselves first and to say their first and last names.

Methods:

Have the students practice introducing themselves by extending a hand and giving a firm handshake. Practice is done first with the teacher, then with each other. Students say, "Hello, my name is Jane Smith, what is your name?" After response, students say, "Nice to meet you."

Extra Practice:

Have a few students from a nearby classroom come into your room and encourage them to practice for 10 minutes with these peers. Students could also go to the administrative offices and introduce themselves to secretaries or administrators. Have the students report results to the teacher and to the rest of the class. Have students discuss their feelings about meeting new people and being the **first to say their first and last names**.

Assignment Sheet:

After role-playing, the teacher passes out assignment sheet #1. Students are instructed to write their names and current date on the paper right away and to keep this sheet in a folder or in a notebook that they keep with them at all times. Instruct them to circle a number each time **they are the first to introduce themselves**. The student must be the initiator with someone new each time and they must be sure to say their first and last names.

Week 2 — Day One

Debriefing Session:

Students report to the teacher and have a brief discussion of their results with assignment sheet #1. The teacher is to give positive feedback to all students and to refrain from reprimanding or scolding anyone who did not do the exercise. This is because the exercises are strictly voluntary and shy students tend to catch on as they see others receiving commendation. The whole group claps as each student gives experiences and shares the number of times they introduced themselves at work or in the community. Students are encouraged to keep up this practice in coming weeks as they meet new people. **Remind them that they are trying to be the first to say something in all exercises. Tell them that they are learning to be friendly at work and at school.**

Lesson 1

Introduce Yourself

Student Name _____ Date _____

Dear Parents, Teachers and Others:

This is our first week of conversation training. Students are learning to be the first to say greetings and to initiate conversations with other people. This is the type of worksheet that will be used by them in coming weeks to record their own actions, gather signatures, or carry out instructions that have been given in the classroom. The student is responsible for circling the numbers each time that an initiation takes place. This sheet is a record of each time the student is the first to introduce himself or herself on the job or in the community.

1   2   3   4   5

1   2   3   4   5

1   2   3   4   5

Lesson 2 Objective
Learn the Names of Your Coworkers & Friends

Week 2 — Day One

Rationale:

Too often young people with disabilities neglect to find out the names of coworkers, schoolmates or community contacts. They need to learn the skill of being the first to introduce themselves.

Objective:

Students will build on lesson one by having a brief review of their skill sheets. Ask students how they introduced themselves. Clap for all students, even shy ones who might not have taken any opportunities to introduce themselves. This is important because they will come around after seeing others take the plunge. Students will now begin to find out names of people of coworkers, schoolmates, administrators and neighbors.

Methods:

Have students practice by introducing themselves to each other, saying their own first and last names and asking the other person's name. Make sure each person acts as the initiator at least once. They say, "Hello, my name is _____, what is your name?"

Extra Practice:

If time permits, **have several high profile peers** from a class nearby come in and allow students to practice. Students might also go to the administration office and practice the introduction and name gathering.

Assignment Sheet:

After role-playing, teacher passes out assignment sheet #2. Students are instructed to write their names and the date on the sheet. This is important because if sheets get dropped or lost, they can be returned to the individual. Explain the sheet to the group and have them mark the first line with the name of the person they either met in class, in another class or in the building. **This exercise is even good for adult learners because many of us might not know the names of all the people we come in contact with daily.** After all, what is the sweetest sound in the human language? Isn't it our own name being used or called by someone? Remind students to use their own first and last names when they introduce themselves.

Week 3 — Day One

Debriefing Session:

Students have had two weeks of social interaction. They should be excited by now. Keep the momentum high now by offering small rewards for those who return sheets and have **something** written on them. Please refrain from scolding or taking anything away from those who are not in the groove yet. They will come around when they see others being commended and being successful! The whole group claps for everyone because these exercises are strictly voluntary and there is no right or wrong involved in this. Each person establishes his/her own norms. Encourage students to keep up the introductions as they meet new people. **Remember they are trying to be the initiator in all exercises.**

Lesson 2

Learn the Names of Your Coworkers & Friends

Student Name _____ Date _____

Please introduce yourself by telling your first and last names. Find out the names of the people you work with and have them sign their names below.

1. Name _____

2. Name _____

3. Name _____

4. Name _____

5. Name _____

6. Name _____

7. Name _____

8. Name _____

9. Name _____

10. Name _____

Lesson 3 Objective
Say Hello: Be the First to Say Hello

Week 3 — Day One

Rationale:

People with disabilities are often shy and lack the self-confidence to approach others and greet them. They are often "acted upon" in conversation and have learned to be passive or responsive to the greetings of others.

Objective:

Students will build on lessons one and two by being the initiator of greetings to people to give them a chance to practice their newly acquired skills. The more greetings they make, the better it is. They need all the practice they can get! This will help to make them stand out at work and in the community. If they remember the names of the people they met, that is a bonus, but the objective now is to get as much practice as possible in being the first to say hello.

Methods:

The teacher asks students to practice being the first to say hello to classmates. They may expand on the hello (e.g., how are you?) but first need to go down the line and be the first to say hello to each classmate.

Extra Practice:

After everyone has had a chance, (about 5 minutes) have students go down the hall of the building initiating hellos to all they meet. **This is difficult, especially if you have students who have a stuttering problem.** Please be patient and allow students to go at their own pace. Some might not do it and that is okay. This should be fun and not a chore. Commend all as they try or succeed. Even a good try is a success. **Try it yourself sometime. If you come within 10 feet of a person, be the first to say hello and you will find out how often we miss doing that.**

Assignment Sheet:

After guided practice and role-playing, have students sign and date the assignment sheet. Go over the assignment thoroughly and make sure students have pencils to carry with them and that they understand where to mark numbers of greetings. Greetings are especially important for the students with severe disabilities. They can do this too with training. If they can say hi, that is sufficient. If they have an augmentative communication device, program it and have them press the button for the greeting. Ask others who are around them if they used the greeting (e.g., bus drivers, other teachers, community helpers).

Week 4 — Day One

Debriefing Session:

Students report about their week of being the first to say hello. Excitement should be high since this was a one-word exercise! The teacher gives positive feedback as each one reports experiences, successes and fears. All should clap as each gives report. These sessions are very important because emotions are running high by now. Everything is voluntary and non-punitive. Students who forget to use the sheet should not be marked down. They will catch up as the momentum builds! Remember, everyone should have at least one circle on the sheet from the introductory practice. Students are encouraged to keep practicing in coming weeks as they meet new people. **Initiation is the key!**

Lesson 3

Say Hello: Be the First to Say Hello

Student Name _____ Date _____

Be the first one to say hello to the people on the job. Every time you are the first one to say hello, circle a number below. If you know the person's name, have them write their name below.

I said hello first:

1   2   3   4   5   6   7   8   9   10

Names of people I said hello to:

1. _____

2. _____

3. _____

4. _____

5. _____

6. _____

7. _____

8. _____

Lesson 4 Objective
Greet the Supervisor/Manager

Week 4 — Day One

Rationale:

People with disabilities need to learn to greet people of authority. This lesson encourages students to be the first to say hello to people in positions of authority. This can be the manager at the work site, the teacher in the classroom, the administrators, the bus drivers or anyone they come in contact with who has authority.

Objective:

This lesson is an expansion on the greeting lessons that have taken place in recent weeks. It might be a little more difficult because the students are greeting people in authority and are going to be the first one to say the greeting. Next, they will seek out these people in the workplace or at school upon arrival. If you are using this lesson in a small group setting, allow students to leave the room and seek out administrators (give them a pass and alert others of the task at hand). **Initiation is key!**

Methods:

The students practice being the first to greet each other. Ask them names of bus drivers, managers, and principals. This is the first time that eye contact is encouraged. Students will practice looking at the person and shaking hands with the initiation of their "hello." If shy students have trouble with eye contact, they may be instructed to look at the persons collar or chin at first instead. **Not many of us look others in the eye as we greet them.** Some people with disabilities even find it painful to make eye contact. Accept whatever attempts you get for eye contact. It will come easier for some than others. If they don't know the names of these people, they will need to take the second step on the assignment sheet and ask for the person's name.

Extra Practice:

If time permits, have students practice being the first to say hello to anyone near the classroom who is in authority (other teachers, media personnel, administrators). Do not mark the assignment sheet with this practice.

Assignment:

After practice sessions, pass out the assignment sheet for lesson #4. Have them put their names and date on the sheet. Explain that they are to be the **first to seek out the boss and to say hello upon arrival**. If they do this once this week, it is sufficient. This is not an easy assignment!

Lesson 4

Greet the Supervisor/Manager

Student Name _____ Date _____

Students are asked to report to the supervisor, say the supervisor's name and greet him/her appropriately. If they do not know the person's name, they need to ask his/her name and have the person sign on the line.

Greet the Supervisor, Boss or Manager

First Workday

Did you greet the supervisor? Yes   No

Name of the supervisor _____

Second Workday

Did you greet the supervisor? Yes   No

Name of the supervisor _____

Week 5
Skills Review Week

Week 5 — Day One — Day Five

Rationale:

This is a big review week. Young people with disabilities **need lots of repetition.** You want these lessons to stick and this week is a chance to review all skills. This accomplishes generalization and carryover. If you have IEP goals regarding appropriate greetings, this is a good time to take data.

Objective:

Students will review the first three lessons this week. At the end of the week please plan to have an awards ceremony. This is called the "Breakfast Meeting." Send the parent notification sheet home asking for specific items each child is to bring for the breakfast meeting. These kinds of activities take place in all work environments and the students will learn how to contribute food items. Invite peers, teachers and administrators involved. High profile peers, like students from the gifted class, can be asked to participate. They can make good mentors because some might be going into future fields that involve people with disabilities (e.g., medical). Have students make a simple invitation. They are the hosts and they will perform their new skills.

Methods:

Invite guests the beginning of the week. Send home parent notification of food items needed. Confirm this the day before the breakfast meeting. Copy the awards certificate for Phase 1 (Pg. 15) and have names filled in for each student. **This is important because the momentum is building and they are being recognized for all of their hard work!**

Extra Practice:

Have a brief session each morning this week reviewing skills. Students can practice with each other and the teacher. When students enter the classroom, wait for greetings to take place. This takes a little time but it's going to pay off!

Assignment:

Use the Skills Review Sheet for this week. Have students write names and dates and explain the sheet in depth. There will be other opportunities to mark skills performed and they might be confused by it. Let the students know that they will be receiving an award for the number of times they use the skills. (This is the first time it becomes a little competitive.) Select appropriate rewards for this (it can be pieces of candy for each response or anything you can give a lot of for little investment). Everyone will still get the certificate regardless of the number of responses.

Awards Ceremony/Breakfast Meeting:

The person who observes the student at the breakfast meeting will also use the Greetings section of the Skills Review Tally to make a mark each time they see the desired initiation. There may not be a lot of initiations at this first meeting. Students need to be guided to offer guests refreshments and to mingle among them. A helper will have a sheet with student names on it and record responses while the teacher helps students work the crowd. This data is important for IEP goals and measurement of student success. **You are gathering data that you can report on later (e.g., John's baseline for saying his first and last name was one time during week one. At week three, John's recorded response for saying his first and last name was six times).**

(Note: Don't try to be the data taker and help students mingle at the same time. You need an independent person to do this for you.)

Skills Review

Introduce Yourself/Learn Names

Be the First to Say Hello/Greet Supervisor

Student Name _____ Date _____

Be the first to speak and circle each time:

Introduce Yourself

1   2   3   4   5   6   7   8   9   10

Learn Names

1   2   3   4   5   6   7   8   9   10

Be the first to Say Hello

1   2   3   4   5   6   7   8   9   10

Greet the Supervisor/Manager

1   2   3   4   5   6   7   8   9   10

Totals

Skills Review

Student Name _____ Date _____

Observer _____ Phase _____

Initiate Greetings	Initiate Questions	Initiate Expansions
Total	Total	Total

Comments

Request for
Breakfast Meeting Items

Dear Parents:

Your child is participating in a breakfast meeting on _____ , _____ as part of the Project for Social Skills training. The breakfast meeting is a chance for them to learn to bring food items to share with peers and to practice their new skills with other people.

Please have your child bring ONE of the following:

○ Donuts

○ Bagels

○ Fruit

○ Muffins

Any other suitable breakfast items

Juice will be provided.

Thank you!

Certificate of Achievement

This certificate is presented to

Say Hello

Completion of Phase 1

_____
Signature

_____
Signature

_____
Date

_____
Date

Lesson 5 Objective
Where Do You Work or Go to School?

Week 6 — Day One

Rationale:

People with disabilities are sometimes unable to articulate the name of their school or work place. This is a conversation that will come up when talking with others.

Objective:

If students are having work experiences in the community they need to be able to say the name of the place where they are working and the school they attend. This helps to build conversation for later interactions in the community. Students will say the name of their school or work place and the street where it is located.

Methods:

Ask each student where they are working or going to school. Some may know by now where they are working but might not know the name of the street. Have all students repeat the name of their location aloud to the teacher and then practice with each other.

Extra Practice:

If these students are not working in the community, have them say the name of the school they attend and where it is located. The exact number of the address is not necessary unless you have students who can do this. Otherwise, the street name is sufficient. Then, you may send students to local administrators to practice telling them the name of the work place or the school. Let administrators and others know by way of a note that students may come to them from time to time with these exercises.

Assignment:

Pass out the assignment sheet for lesson five and have students put names and dates on the page. Instruct the students that they will find out where they work and write its name on the first line. They will write the street name or address on the second line. They are then asked to be the initiator in telling someone where they work or go to school.

Week Seven — Day One

Debriefing Session:

Ask students to show their sheets from lesson #5 and have them tell once again the name and location of assignment. Commend students for their efforts by having them all clap for each individual.

Self-Managed Checklist

Lesson 5

"Where Do You Work?"

Student Name _____ Date _____

Be the first to say the name of the place where you work.
When you tell people where you work, circle a number.

1   2   3   4   5

I Work:

Name: _____

Street: _____

Self-Managed
Checklist

Lesson 5

"Where Do You Go to School?"

Student Name _____ Date _____

Be the first to say the name of your school. When you tell people where you go to school, circle a number. Write the name of your school and the name of the street where your school is located.

1   2   3   4   5

My School:

Name: _____

Street: _____

Time Allotted: 25 minutes

Lesson 6 Objective
Ask Questions: How Are You Today?

Week 7 — Day One

Rationale:
Some people with disabilities do not ask enough questions.

Objective:
Students will be given a repertoire of appropriate questions that they can use at work and in the community. These are common questions that are often used by people in the workplace and in the community. The main objective is for the students to begin to build their repertoires and be the initiator of appropriate questions.

Methods:
Students practice being the first to greet and say, "Hello _____ how are you today?" They then give their partner a chance to respond. If they expand on the conversation, that is fine but it is not necessary. They are instructed to use the name of the person in the greeting. They can role play with the teacher and each other.

Extra Practice:
Bring in students from class nearby and have your students practice with them. If you have students who are doing any type of community service credits, they can count the time as part of their community service. Administrators or teachers in the vicinity can function as partners as well. The more people they meet that they do not know, the better it is. By now, eye contact should be improving as a natural consequence of their people-contacts. Remind them of this but note that this is not critical right now.

Assignment:
Pass out assignment sheets for the question, "How are you?" Have them put their names and date on the paper (for papers that are dropped or lost). If students are behind in the lessons at this point, encourage them to catch up. They can jump in at this point but the other lessons are a real foundation for their confidence and progress. You might not be able to keep everyone together and it will get tricky to keep them all practicing in the weekly sessions. If need be, you can catch these students up during the review week.

Lesson 6

Be the First to Ask a Question: "How Are You Today?"

Student Name _____ Date _____

Be the first to ask people on the job, in your school, or in your community how they are doing. Circle a number after you ask the question and ask them to sign on the line.

I asked the question, "How Are You Today?"

1   2   3   4   5

Names of the people that I asked the question:

1. _____

2. _____

3. _____

4. _____

5. _____

Lessons 7-17 Objective
Learn to Ask Questions: Be the First to Ask a Question

Lessons 7 - 17 — Day One

Rationale:

If given an appropriate repertoire of questions, people with disabilities will ask appropriate questions.

Objective:

To give students a repertoire of appropriate questions so they can initiate conversations with coworkers, classmates, school personnel and others. They must be the initiator of the predetermined questions and wait for a response. Lessons seven through seventeen are all the same and involve asking a single-sentence question. Try to give everyone the same questions each day. This lesson is done twice weekly because of its importance.

Methods:

Students will practice two single-sentence questions, preferably two days apart. Give them only one question at a time, even if you have to stretch these lessons out longer than the number of weeks that is forecasted. This is the core of the training and everything else will build on this core, so take your time. These questions have been formulated for the workplace based on observations of what workers ask one another. If your students are not in the work place yet, please feel free to adapt the questions for their present environment. Tell the students what the question is and have them practice with you one-on-one. After each has had a turn with you, have them practice with each other.

Extra Practice:

This is a great time to videotape each student. Criteria for mastery is five questions initiated in a five minute period. This is a goal that all can eventually reach (results of field-testing shows that even students with severe disabilities can master five initiations with cues). Pair students with an unfamiliar person alone in a room and ask them to talk "normally." Get a sympathetic person who will talk with the students for five minutes and ask them to have a conversation. Don't tell the partner what you are looking for, other than helping students learn to talk to people in the community.

Assignment:

The next ten assignments sheets are exactly the same and will give students a chance to get a lot of practice in. Ask three people the same question in a given day and ask the student to verify that they were the first one to ask the question. The first assignment sheet is a review of the question, "How Are You?" It serves to get everyone off to a successful start.

Debriefing Sessions for Lessons 7 - 17:

All debriefing sessions should be positive and upbeat. Have each student give their experiences with asking questions. All clap as each student gives theirs.

Breakfast Meeting for Lessons 7 - 17:

Hold a breakfast meeting for these lessons at the end of the week after #17 is completed. There will be the usual review lessons that week which culminate in the breakfast meeting. Don't skip the breakfast meetings because your certificates are given out for Phase 2 (Pg. 42).

Lesson 7

Learn to Ask Questions:
Be the First to Ask a Question

Student Name _____ Date _____

Be the first to ask your coworkers and friends how they are doing today.
When you ask the question, circle a number and have them sign on the line.

1   2   3   4   5

Names of people who told me how they were doing today:

1. _____

2. _____

3. _____

4. _____

5. _____

Lesson 8

Be the First to Ask a Question:
"How Is Your Family?"

Student Name _____ Date _____

Be the first to ask your Coworkers and friends about their families. When you ask the question, circle a number and have them sign on the line.

1   2   3   4   5

Names of people who told me how their families were:

1. _____

2. _____

3. _____

4. _____

5. _____

Lesson 9

Be the First to Ask a Question: "How is Your Day Going?"

Student Name _____ Date _____

Be the first to ask your coworkers and friends how their day is going. Do not forget to wait for the answer to the question. Circle a number and have the person sign on the line.

1   2   3   4   5

Names of people who told me about their day:

1. _____

2. _____

3. _____

4. _____

5. _____

Skills Review

Be the First to Ask a Question

Student Name _____ Date _____

Be the first to ask a question and circle each time:

How Are You Today?

1   2   3   4   5   6   7   8   9   10

How is Your Family?

1   2   3   4   5   6   7   8   9   10

How is Your Day Going?

1   2   3   4   5   6   7   8   9   10

Certificate of Achievement

This certificate is presented to

Mini Certificate for Completion of Skills Review

_____
Signature

_____
Date

_____
Signature

_____
Date

Self-Managed
Checklist

Lesson 10

Be the First To Ask a Question:
"What Time Do You Go Home Today?"

Student Name _____ Date _____

Be the first to ask your coworkers what time they go home each day.
When you ask the question, circle a number and have them sign on the line.

1   2   3   4   5

Names of people who told me what time they go home:

1. _____

2. _____

3. _____

4. _____

5. _____

Lesson 11

Be the First to Ask a Question:
"How Do You Like the Weather Today?"

Student Name _____ Date _____

Be the first to ask your coworkers and friends how they like the weather today. When you ask the question, circle a number and have them sign on the line.

1   2   3   4   5

Names of people who told me how they like the weather today:

1. _____

2. _____

3. _____

4. _____

5. _____

Lesson 12

Be the First to Ask a Question: "What Did You Do Last Night?"

Student Name _____ Date _____

Be the first to ask your coworkers and friends and friends what they did last night. When you ask the question, circle a number and have them sign on the line.

1   2   3   4   5

Names of people who told me what they did last night:

1. _____

2. _____

3. _____

4. _____

5. _____

Skills Review

Be the First to Ask a Question

Student Name _____ Date _____

Be the first to ask a question and circle each time:

What Time Do You Go Home Today?

1   2   3   4   5   6   7   8   9   10

How Do You Like the Weather Today?

1   2   3   4   5   6   7   8   9   10

What Did You Do Last Night?

1   2   3   4   5   6   7   8   9   10

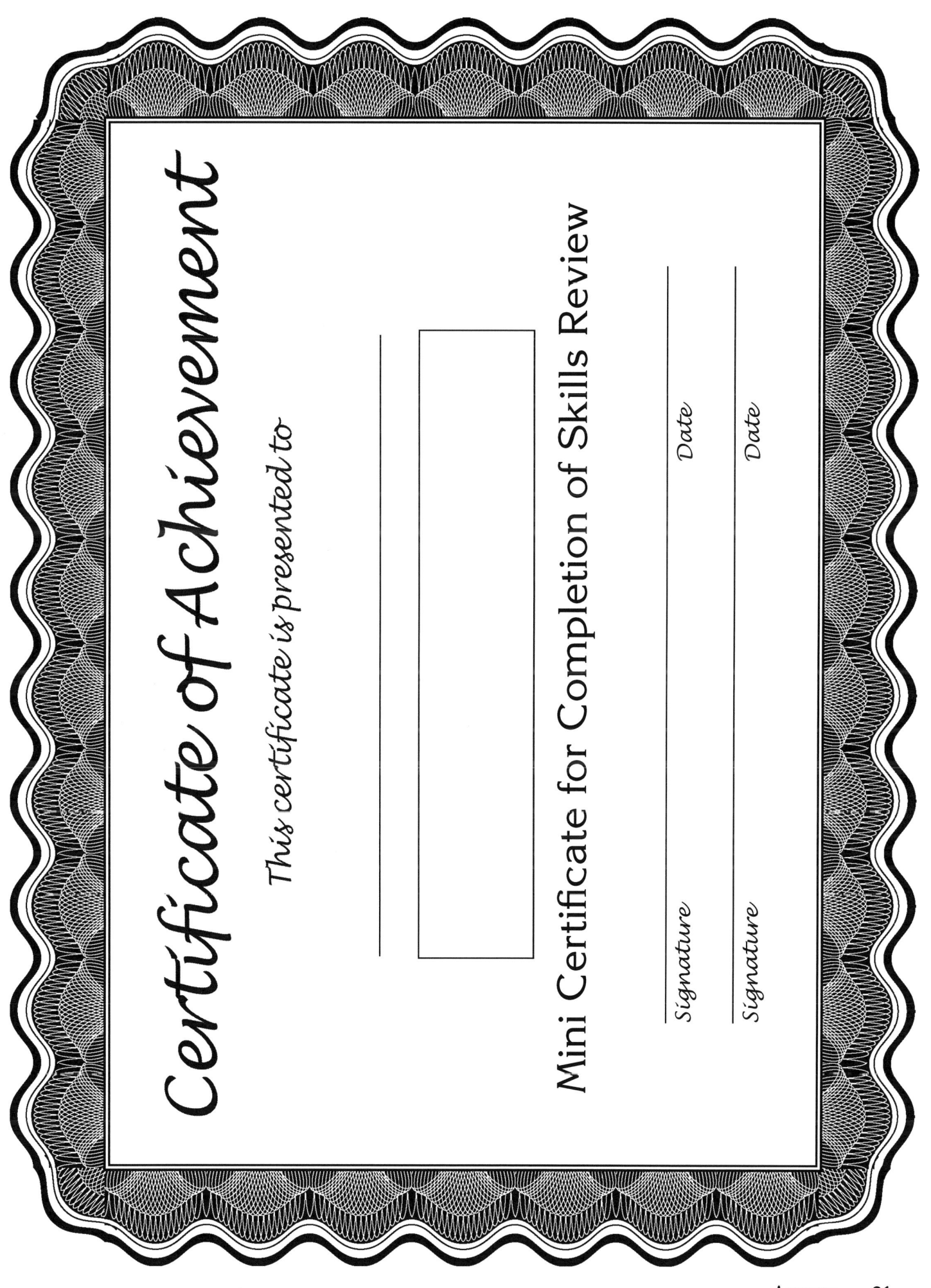

Certificate of Achievement

This certificate is presented to

Mini Certificate for Completion of Skills Review

_____ Signature

_____ Date

_____ Signature

_____ Date

Lesson 13

Be the First to Ask a Question:
"What is Your Favorite TV Show?"

Student Name _____ Date _____

Be the first to ask your coworkers and friends what their favorite TV show is. When you ask the question, circle a number and have them sign on the line.

1   2   3   4   5

Names of people who told me their favorite show:

1. _____

2. _____

3. _____

4. _____

5. _____

Lesson 14

Be the First to Ask a Question: "How Was Your Weekend?"

Student Name _____ Date _____

Be the first to ask your coworkers and friends how they enjoyed their weekend. After you ask the question, circle a number and have them sign on the line.

1   2   3   4   5

People who told me about their weekend:

1. _____

2. _____

3. _____

4. _____

5. _____

Lesson 15

Be the First to Ask a Question: "Do You Have Any Pets?"

Student Name _____ Date _____

Be the first to ask your coworkers and friends if they have a pet.
After you ask the question, circle a number and have them sign on the line.

1　　　2　　　3　　　4　　　5

Names of people who told me they have pets:

1. _____

2. _____

3. _____

4. _____

5. _____

Skills Review

Be the First to Ask a Question

Student Name _____ Date _____

Be the first to ask a question and circle each time:

What is you favorite TV show?

1   2   3   4   5   6   7   8   9   10

How was your weekend?

1   2   3   4   5   6   7   8   9   10

Do you have any pets?

1   2   3   4   5   6   7   8   9   10

Certificate of Achievement

This certificate is presented to

Mini Certificate for Completion of Skills Review

_____
Signature

_____
Date

_____
Signature

_____
Date

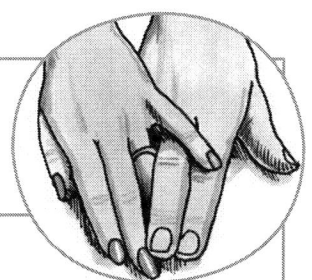

Lesson 16

Be the First to Ask a Question: "Are You Married?"

Student Name _____ Date _____

Be the first to ask a coworker if they are married. After you ask the question, circle a number and have them sign on the line.

1   2   3   4   5

People who told me whether they are married:

1. _____

2. _____

3. _____

4. _____

5. _____

Lesson 17

Be the First to Ask a Question: "Do You Have Any Children?"

Student Name _____ Date _____

Be the first to ask your coworkers and friends if they have any children. After you ask the question, circle a number and have them sign on the line.

1   2   3   4   5

People who told me whether they have any children:

1. _____

2. _____

3. _____

4. _____

5. _____

Skills Review

Be the First to Ask a Question

Student Name _____ Date _____

Be the first to ask a question and circle each time:

Are You Married?

1   2   3   4   5   6   7   8   9   10

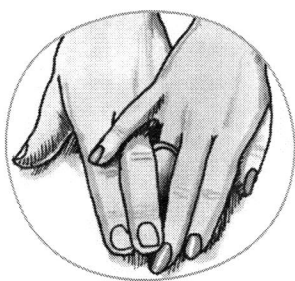

Do You Have Any Children?

1   2   3   4   5   6   7   8   9   10

Breakfast Meeting

Skills Review

Rationale:

People with disabilities require repetition to retain skills. This review week will focus on students asking as many questions as possible.

Objective:

To review the lessons on asking questions. Students are to ask as many of the questions in the repertoire as possible.

Methods:

Students are to practice asking questions in the classroom with each other and the teacher. Students are encouraged to ask at least five questions during the practice sessions. Practice sessions should take place each morning if possible.

Assignments:

Pass out assignment sheets each day with three questions on each sheet. Please refer to page 35 for the Skills Review questions. If you are in a regular classroom setting, the teacher has the students debrief each morning to report on the questions they asked. Ask them if they were the initiators of the questions. Then ask all to clap and commend each other for their efforts.

Breakfast Meeting:

This is the week of the breakfast meeting. Pass out the requests to parents for breakfast items and invite high profile peers to the breakfast meeting. Use the data sheets to have a third party helper record responses of students during the breakfast meeting. (Please refer to page 12 for the Skills Review Sheet and use the sections on Greetings and Questions. Give this Review Sheet to the person who observes the students at the Breakfast Meeting to chart their performances).
Data may be recorded by simply making a mark when an initiation is observed. Note any other usage of conversation that is in the repertoire during the breakfast meeting. This is a good time to reward the students for their efforts. Inexpensive stuffed animals, candy, fruits, or times from the dollar store can be used as incentives this week. The atmosphere should be festive and positive for all. After the breakfast meeting, let students know how many responses the observer noted and commend them with praise and incentives.

Totals

Skills Review

Student Name _____ Date _____

Observer _____ Phase _____

Initiate Greetings	Initiate Questions	Initiate Expansions
Total	Total	Total

Comments

Certificate of Achievement

This certificate is presented to

Be the First to Ask a Question

Completion of Phase 2

_____
Signature

_____
Date

_____
Signature

_____
Date

Holiday Skills

Review

Rationale:
Students will have many opportunities to practice their conversational interactions skills while on a holiday. They can use the skills at home, at church, and in the community.

Objective:
To promote generalization and carryover of acquired skills across the environment. This will promote use of skills during holiday periods.

Methods:
Explain to students that they are going to use their new skills during the holiday period. They will continue to introduce themselves, and be the first to say hello and to ask questions. Parents and friends are asked to notice when skills are used and to write a note to the teacher regarding the use of the skills. Be sure that parents understand that the student is to be the initiator of the conversation.

Assignment:
Explain the holiday practice to the students and be sure they understand that parents will be listening for the use of their new skills. The picture cues will serve as a reminder to the student to use the new skills.

Holiday Skills

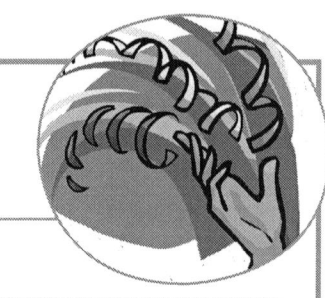

Review

Student Name _____ Date _____

Dear Parents and Friends:

Our students have come a long way in their initiations of conversation.
We are asking you to notice whether your student is the first to greet others, to introduce themselves by saying their first and last names, to ask how people are doing, how their families are doing, and how they like the weather.
They have also learned get-acquainted questions about pets, marriage, children, weekend activities, and favorite TV shows. Please remind the students of the questions and write a note to the teacher. Please sign this note and return it to the teacher after the holidays.

Note From Parent/Friend:

_____

_____

_____

_____

_____

_____

_____

_____

Signature_____ Date _____

Lessons 18-28 Objective
Expansion Questions

Lessons #18 - 28 — Day One

Rationale:

People with disabilities often use short expressions and do not expand on those short expressions.

Objective:

To give students opportunities to expand on the one-sentence questions they have in their repertoire. Lessons #18 through #28 are all the same pattern. The lessons involve two one-sentence questions that are related and are initiated by the students.

Methods:

Students will practice two single-sentence questions at the beginning of the week. These two questions will be the practice questions for the entire week. Some students will naturally expand on the questions with their own expressions and that is OK. Most of the students will be adding to their repertoire and will need help to ask the expansion questions. Go over the questions with the students and have each student repeat both questions. Students will practice with the teacher first and then with each other.

Extra Practice:

This is a good time to make another videotape for assessment purposes. The expansion questions will eventually be counted as part of the criteria of five initiations in a five-minute period when the course is completed. Pair the students in a quiet environment and tape them talking to an unfamiliar person. The partner is told to just have a conversation and allow the student to talk "normally." Do not tell the partner what you are looking for. Say simply that you are helping students to learn to talk to people in the community.

Assignment:

The next ten assignments sheets are basically the same and will give the students a chance to get in a lot of good practice. They will ask people the two expansion questions and record the number of people by circling the number. It's not absolutely necessary that they get the person's name this time around but rather to have the person record whether the student was the first one to ask the question. The expansion questions are placed in reverse order from the most recent back to the first, "How Are You Today?"

Debriefing Sessions for Lessons #18 - 28:

All debriefing sessions should be very positive with lots of verbal praise. Allow each student to express his or her triumphs, fears, etc. All should clap as each student gives experiences. At this point, students should have collected quite a notebook of lessons they have completed. If they have lost some lessons or failed to complete some lessons, do not scold them. This is designed to be completely voluntary and non-punitive in nature. The students who fall behind can always repeat the course next year.

Breakfast Meeting:

The breakfast meeting for this phase will take place at the end of week twenty-eight. This is when certificates will be given out for phase three of the course. You might be heading for another holiday period at the end of this part of the course and the note to parents should be used at that time for generalization and carryover.

Self-Managed Checklist

Lesson 18

Be the First to Ask Two Expansion Questions:

"Do You Have Any Children?"

"How Many Children Do You Have?"

Student Name _____ Date _____

Be the first to ask your coworkers if they have any children. After you ask the questions, circle a number and have the person write whether you were the first to ask the questions.

Do You Have Any Children?

1   2   3   4   5

How Many Children Do You Have?

1   2   3   4   5

1. Was the student the first to ask you the questions?	Yes	No
2. Was the student the first to ask you the questions?	Yes	No
3. Was the student the first to ask you the questions?	Yes	No
4. Was the student the first to ask you the questions?	Yes	No
5. Was the student the first to ask you the questions?	Yes	No

Lesson 19

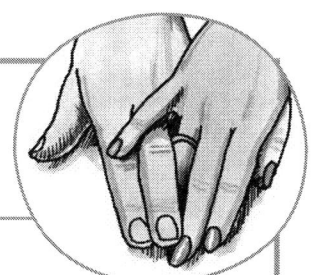

Be the First to Ask Two Expansion Questions:

"Are You Married?"

"How Long Have You Been Married?"

Student Name _____ Date _____

Be the first to ask a coworker if they are married and if so, how long they have been married. If they are not married, you do not need to ask the second question. Have the person write whether you were the first to ask the questions.

Are You Married?

1   2   3   4   5

How Long Have You Been Married?

1   2   3   4   5

1.	Was the student the first to ask the questions?	Yes	No
2.	Was the student the first to ask the questions?	Yes	No
3.	Was the student the first to ask the questions?	Yes	No
4.	Was the student the first to ask the questions?	Yes	No
5.	Was the student the first to ask the questions?	Yes	No

Lesson 20

Be the First to Ask Two Expansion Questions:

"Do You Have Any Pets?"

"How Many Pets do You Have?"

Student Name _____ Date _____

Be the first to ask your coworkers and friends if they have any pets and how many pets they have. After you ask the questions, circle a number and have the person write whether you were the first to ask the questions.

Do You Have Any Pets?

1   2   3   4   5

How Many Pets Do You Have?

1   2   3   4   5

1. Was the student the first to ask you the questions?	Yes	No
2. Was the student the first to ask you the questions?	Yes	No
3. Was the student the first to ask you the questions?	Yes	No
4. Was the student the first to ask you the questions?	Yes	No
5. Was the student the first to ask you the questions?	Yes	No

Lesson 21

Be the First to Ask Two Expansion Questions:

"How Was Your Weekend?"

"What Did You Do Last Weekend?"

Student Name _____ Date _____

Be the first to ask coworkers and friends how they enjoyed their weekend and what they did last weekend. After you ask the questions circle a number and have the person write whether you were the first to ask the questions.

How Was Your Weekend?

1   2   3   4   5

What Did You Do Last Weekend?

1   2   3   4   5

1. Was the student the first to ask you the questions?	Yes	No
2. Was the student the first to ask you the questions?	Yes	No
3. Was the student the first to ask you the questions?	Yes	No
4. Was the student the first to ask you the questions?	Yes	No
5. Was the student the first to ask you the questions?	Yes	No

Lesson 22

Be the First to Ask Two Expansion Questions:

"What is Your Favorite TV Show?"

"When Do You Watch Your Favorite TV Show?"

Student Name _____ Date _____

Be the first to ask Coworkers and friends the name of their favorite TV show and when they watch the show. After you ask the questions, circle a number and have the person write whether you were the first to ask the questions.

What Is Your Favorite TV Show?

1   2   3   4   5

When Do You Watch Your Favorite TV Show?

1   2   3   4   5

1. Was the student the first to ask the question?	Yes	No
2. Was the student the first to ask the question?	Yes	No
3. Was the student the first to ask the question?	Yes	No
4. Was the student the first to ask the question?	Yes	No
5. Was the student the first to ask the question?	Yes	No

Lesson 23

Be the First Two
Expansion Questions:

"What Did You Do Last Night?"

"Did You Stay At Home?"

Student Name _____ Date _____

Be the first to ask your coworkers and friends what they did last night and if they stayed at home. When you ask the questions, circle a number and have the person write whether you were the first to ask the questions.

What Did You Do Last Night?

1   2   3   4   5

Did You Stay At Home?

1   2   3   4   5

1. Was the student the first to ask the questions?	Yes	No
2. Was the student the first to ask the questions?	Yes	No
3. Was the student the first to ask the questions?	Yes	No
4. Was the student the first to ask the questions?	Yes	No
5. Was the student the first to ask the questions?	Yes	No

Self-Managed Checklist

Lesson 24

Be the First to Ask Two Expansion Questions:

"What Time Do You Go Home Today?"

"What Will You Do When You Get Home?"

Student Name _____ Date _____

Be the first to ask your coworkers what time they go home today and what will they do when they get home. When you ask the questions, circle a number and have the person write whether you were the first to ask the questions.

What Time Do You Go Home Today?

1   2   3   4   5

What Will You Do When You Get Home?

1   2   3   4   5

1. Was the student the first to ask the questions?	Yes	No
2. Was the student the first to ask the questions?	Yes	No
3. Was the student the first to ask the questions?	Yes	No
4. Was the student the first to ask the questions?	Yes	No
5. Was the student the first to ask the questions?	Yes	No

Self-Managed Checklist

Lesson 25

Be the First to Ask Two
Expansion Questions:

"How is Your Day Going?"

"Are You Having a Nice Day?"

Student Name _____ Date _____

Be the first to ask friends and coworkers how their day is going and if they are having a nice day. When you ask the questions, circle a number and have the person write whether you were the first one to ask the questions.

How Is Your Day Going?

1   2   3   4   5

Are You Having A Nice Day?

1   2   3   4   5

1. Was the student the first to ask the questions?	Yes	No
2. Was the student the first to ask the questions?	Yes	No
3. Was the student the first to ask the questions?	Yes	No
4. Was the student the first to ask the questions?	Yes	No
5. Was the student the first to ask the questions?	Yes	No

Lesson 26

Be the First to Ask Two Expansion Questions:

"How Is Your Family?"

"Is Everyone Doing OK?"

Student Name _____ Date _____

Be the first to ask Coworkers and friends how their families are doing and if they are OK. When you ask the questions, circle a number and have the person write whether you were the first one to ask the questions.

How Is Your Family?

1 2 3 4 5

Is Everyone Doing OK?

1 2 3 4 5

1. Was the student the first to ask the questions?	Yes	No
2. Was the student the first to ask the questions?	Yes	No
3. Was the student the first to ask the questions?	Yes	No
4. Was the student the first to ask the questions?	Yes	No
5. Was the student the first to ask the questions?	Yes	No

Lesson 27

Be the First to Ask Two Expansion Questions:

"How Are You Today?"

"Are You Feeling OK?"

Student Name _____ Date _____

Be the first to ask Coworkers and friends how they are doing and if they are OK. After you ask the questions, circle a number and have the person write whether you were the first one to ask the questions.

How Are You Today?

1   2   3   4   5

Are You Doing OK?

1   2   3   4   5

1. Was the student the first to ask the questions?	Yes	No
2. Was the student the first to ask the questions?	Yes	No
3. Was the student the first to ask the questions?	Yes	No
4. Was the student the first to ask the questions?	Yes	No
5. Was the student the first to ask the questions?	Yes	No

Breakfast Meeting
Skills Review

Rationale:

People with disabilities require much repetition in order to retain skills. This review week will focus on students asking as many expansion question as possible.

Objective:

To review lessons on asking expansion questions. Students are to ask as many of the questions in the repertoire as possible.

Methods:

Students are to practice asking questions in the classroom with each other and the teacher. Students are encouraged to ask at least five of the two-sentence expansion questions during the practice sessions. Practice sessions should take place each morning if possible.

Assignments:

Pass out assignment sheets each day with two expansion questions on each sheet. (Lessons 28-32). If you are in a traditional classroom setting, the teacher will debrief students each morning and have students report on the questions they asked. Ask students if they were the initiator of the questions. All to clap and commend each other for their efforts.

Breakfast Meeting:

The breakfast meeting will take place on day five or six (there are enough review sheets for five days practice). Pass out the requests for breakfast items at the beginning of the week. (Refer to page 62). Invite high profile peers or administrators to attend the breakfast meeting. Use the data sheets to record the responses of the students during the breakfast meeting. Note any other usage of the repertoire during the breakfast meeting. Certificates for Phase 3 (Pg. 64) — Asking Two Expansion Questions sheets are to be given out at the end of the breakfast meeting. Other rewards can also be given at this time for their efforts. The atmosphere is to be festive and positive for all. After the breakfast meeting, let students know how many responses the observer noted and commend them for their efforts.

Lesson 28

Skills Review

Student Name _____ Date _____

Be the first to ask your coworkers if they have any children and how many children they have. After you ask the questions, have the person circle whether you were the first to ask the questions.

Do you have any children?

1   2

How many children do you have?

1   2

1. Was the student the first to ask you the questions?   Yes   No
2. Was the student the first to ask you the questions?   Yes   No

Are you married?

1   2

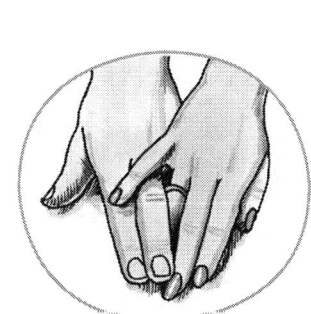

How long have you been married?

1   2

1. Was the student the first to ask you the questions?   Yes   No
2. Was the student the first to ask you the questions?   Yes   No

Lesson 29

Skills Review

Student Name _____ Date _____

Be the first to ask your coworkers and friends if they have any pets and how many pets they have. After you ask the questions, circle a number and have the person circle whether you were the first to ask the questions.

Do you have any pets?

1   2

How may pets do you have?

1   2

1. Was the student the first to ask you the questions?   Yes   No
2. Was the student the first to ask you the questions?   Yes   No

How was your weekend?

1   2

What did you do last weekend?

1   2

1. Was the student the first to ask you the questions?   Yes   No
2. Was the student the first to ask you the questions?   Yes   No

Lesson 30

Skills Review

Student Name _____ Date _____

Be the first to ask your coworkers and friends what their favorite TV show is and when do they watch it. After you ask the questions, circle a number and have the person circle whether you were the first to ask the questions.

What is your favorite TV show?

1   2

When do you watch your favorite TV show?

1   2

1. Was the student the first to ask you the questions?   Yes   No
2. Was the student the first to ask you the questions?   Yes   No

What did you do last night?

1   2

Did you stay at home?

1   2

1. Was the student the first to ask you the questions?   Yes   No
2. Was the student the first to ask you the questions?   Yes   No

Lesson 31

Skills Review

Student Name _____ Date _____

Be the first to ask your coworkers and friends what time they go home today and what will they do when they get home. After you ask the questions, circle a number and have the person circle whether you were the first to ask the questions.

What time will you go home today?

1   2

What will you do when you get home?

1   2

1. Was the student the first to ask you the questions?   Yes   No
2. Was the student the first to ask you the questions?   Yes   No

How is you day going?

1   2

Are you having a nice day?

1   2

1. Was the student the first to ask you the questions?   Yes   No
2. Was the student the first to ask you the questions?   Yes   No

Lesson 32

Skills Review

Student Name _____ Date _____

Be the first to ask your coworkers and friends how they are today and are they feeling OK. After you ask the questions, circle a number and have the person circle whether you were the first to ask the questions.

How are you today?

1   2

Are you feeling OK?

1   2

1. Was the student the first to ask you the questions?   Yes   No
2. Was the student the first to ask you the questions?   Yes   No

How is your family?

1   2

Is everyone doing OK?

1   2

1. Was the student the first to ask you the questions?   Yes   No
2. Was the student the first to ask you the questions?   Yes   No

Request for Breakfast Meeting Items

Dear Parents:

Your child is participating in a breakfast meeting on _____ , _____ as part of the **Conversation Skills** training. The breakfast meeting is a chance for them to learn to bring food items to share with peers and to practice their new skills with other people.

Please have your child bring ONE of the following:

○ Donuts

○ Bagels

○ Fruit

○ Muffins

Any other suitable breakfast items

Juice will be provided.

Thank you!

Totals

Skills Review

Student Name _____ Date _____

Observer _____ Phase _____

Initiate Greetings	Initiate Questions	Initiate Expansions
Total	Total	Total

Comments

Certificate of Achievement

This certificate is presented to

_____

Be the First to Ask two Expansion Questions

Completion of Phase 3

_____ Date

_____
Signature

_____ Date

_____
Signature

Lesson 33 - 35 Objective
Social Amenities

Rationale:

People with disabilities sometimes need help with social amenities. They might miss social cues that call for responses that most of us take for granted, like please and thank-you. They may receive compliments well but might not be able to generate compliments on their own.

Objective:

To provide students with commonly used social amenities.

Methods:

Give students concrete examples of situations in which they might use please and thank-you. For example, "please give me _____."

Another example is, "Thank-you for helping me _____." "I like your tie today." Other examples of compliments students can learn are, "you look nice today," "you have a nice smile" or, "you are so helpful."

Some students have these social courtesies down pat and will need little help, while others will need more practice. If the teacher has noticed students who need more help, these students can be paired to practice with others who do not need as much help with this exercise. Give students a chance to role-play with each other at least three times. Students can practice the "please" by asking for other students to give them something that is visible in the room. The student can then respond by saying thank-you. The teacher might ask students to name situations where please and thank-you is needed. The teacher can demonstrate appropriate situations and compliments. These lessons are done separately, one each week.

Assignment:

Pass out the assignment sheet for saying please and have students put name and date on it. Explain to them that they are going to be on the look out for chances to say please and to record it on the sheet. The object of these lessons is to make students more aware of this amenity and to use it.

Debriefing Sessions for Lessons 33 - 35:

Encourage students to relate their experiences with saying please and thank-you and giving compliments. Comment on how many times each student used the amenities. Talk about the different situations that called for please and thank-you. Talk about situations that can be used to give compliments. Commend all for their efforts and have all clap after each student gives experiences.

Lesson 33

Social Amenities:

Be the First to Say "Thank-you!"

Student Name _____ Date _____

Be the first to say "thank-you" to your teachers, friends, family and coworkers. After you remember to be the first to say thank-you, circle a number. If you know the names of the people you said thank-you to, write their names or have them write their own names on the line.

I said "thank-you":

1   2   3   4   5   6   7   8   9   10

Names of people I thanked:

1 _____

2. _____

3. _____

4. _____

Self-Managed Checklist

Lesson 34

Social Amenities:

Be the First to Say "Please!"

Student Name _____ Date _____

Be the first to say "please" to your teachers, friends, family and coworkers. Circle a number every time you say the word, please. If you know the person's name, write their names on the line or have them write their own names on the line.

I said "Please":

1   2   3   4   5   6   7   8   9   10

Names of people I said "please" to:

1. _____

2. _____

3. _____

4. _____

Self-Managed Checklist

Lesson 35

Social Amenities:

Be the First to Give a Compliment

Student Name _____ Date _____

Be the first to give someone a compliment. Tell the person something nice. Circle a number each time you give a compliment and have the person write his/her name on the line.

I gave a compliment:

1   2   3   4   5

1. _____

2. _____

3. _____

4. _____

5. _____

Lesson 35A

Social Amenities:

Be the First to say "Thank You!"

Student Name _____ Date _____

Be the first to say "thank you" to your friends and family. Circle a number each time you give a compliment and have the person write his/her name on the line.

I said "thank you":

1   2   3   4   5

1. _____

2. _____

3. _____

4. _____

5. _____

Lesson 35B

Social Amenities:

Be the First to Say "Please!"

Student Name _____ Date _____

Be the first to say "please" to your friends and family. Circle a number each time you say please and have the person write his/her name on the line.

I said "please":

1   2   3   4   5

1. _____

2. _____

3. _____

4. _____

5. _____

Skills Review

Social Amenities:

Be the First to Say "Please!" and "Thank You!"

Give a Compliment

Student Name _____ Date _____

Be the first to use your new skills of please, thank you and giving compliments. Circle a number each time you use your new skills.

I said "please":

1   2   3   4   5   6   7   8   9   10

I said "thank you":

1   2   3   4   5   6   7   8   9   10

I gave a compliment:

1   2   3   4   5   6   7   8   9   10

Request for Breakfast Meeting Items

Dear Parents:

Your child is participating in a breakfast meeting on _____ , _____ as part of the **Conversation Skills** training. The breakfast meeting is a chance for them to learn to bring food items to share with peers and to practice their new skills with other people.

Please have your child bring ONE of the following:

○ Donuts

○ Bagels

○ Fruit

○ Muffins

Any other suitable breakfast items

Juice will be provided.

Thank you!

Skills Review

Totals

Student Name _____ Date _____

Observer _____ Phase _____

Initiate Greetings	Initiate Questions	Initiate Expansions
Total	Total	Total

Comments

Breakfast Meeting
Social Amenities/Skills Review

Rationale:

This week is devoted to the skills review and culminates in the breakfast meeting. A young person with disabilities needs lots of repetition. You want the lessons to stick and this is a chance to review all skills learned so far. This is the time to see if you've achieved generalization and carryover. If you have IEP goals regarding appropriate greetings, this is a good time to take data.

Methods:

Use the Breakfast Meeting Invitation to invite those who have been a part of the training so far. Have students deliver the invitations to communication partners in the school. Send the Breakfast Meeting announcements to homes so that caregivers can donate foods items. If you would like to, assign specific items to certain students. These announcements and invitations will go out at the beginning of the week.

Extra Practice:

Have students deliver invitations to peers, teachers and administrators in the school. Have them practice introducing themselves as they pass out the invitations to others, and again when they offer the invitations to arriving invitees.

Data Recording:

Be sure to designate someone as a third party recorder of all responses during the Breakfast Meeting. This is a social event that teaches the students to share food items with others and to practice their skills in a relaxed atmosphere. Use the data-recording sheet to record all responses. Look for greetings, initiation of questions, social amenities, and use of names of familiar people. Social amenities may be recorded under the Greetings section of the Skills Review Sheet. It's fine to structure the event so that students can use their skills. This structure can be brought about by asking them to introduce themselves, encouraging them to ask appropriate questions, and to employ their newly acquired social amenities.

Debriefing After the Breakfast Meeting:

After the breakfast meeting is over, share the results of responses with all of the students. If you have a simple tangible reward to offer to all for their efforts, give it at this time. You may offer stuffed animals, fruit gifts, or candy and gum. If you have a classroom store, you might allow the students to purchase items according to their responses. This is a time of celebration and everyone should be congratulated for his or her responses. Clap for all as responses that are read.

Lesson 36 Objective
Conversation Partners

Rationale:

People with disabilities are often lonely on the job and in the community. Soliciting the help of natural supporters can forge friendships and productive work relationships.

Methods:

Now that your students have become social butterflies, it is time to give them lots of practice in a natural setting with one person. If you are in a school, you might solicit the help of high-profile peers who need community service hours. If you are on the job, ask managers/supervisors for names of employees who would not mind spending five minutes of their break/lunch time with the student trainee. The students will execute weekly lessons with their partner during a five-minute conversation period. The reward for the partner can be certificates of appreciation for a service rendered to the community. Most people do not mind doing this and begin to really enjoy the community of the partner with disabilities. If you can't find anyone who will spend the five-minute period, have students go down the hall to administrators, secretaries, or media personnel to execute the lessons. This is fine as long as it is the same person each week.

Assignments:

The next assignments are basically the same and will give the students a chance to get a lot of good quality practice. If they are on the job, they will ask the break partner what time they can meet them for a short break. Be sure to explain ahead of time that the person does not have to spend his/her entire break period with the student unless they really want to. The five-minute period is plenty of time to execute the lesson and to forge a bond between the parties involved. These lessons will promote carryover and generalization for all of the weeks of study that have gone on before this. Some of the lessons are sessions review and some are new ones.
Use the role-play methods with which students are already familiar to teach the lessons.

Lesson 36

What is Your Partner's Name?

What Is the Best Time to Meet Your Partner?

Student Name _____ Date _____

Introduce yourself to your partner and ask your partner to tell you his/her name.

I Introduced Myself   Yes   No

I Asked My Partner His/Her Name?   Yes   No

My Partner's Name Is _____

Ask your partner for the best time to meet and talk.

The Best Time For My Partner Is _____

Lesson 37

Be the First to Give Your Partner a Compliment

Student Name _____ Date _____

When you talk with your partner today, give your partner a compliment. After you compliment your partner, circle that you did it and have your partner sign on the line.

I gave my partner a compliment   Yes   No

Partner's Signature _____

Lesson 38

Be the First to Ask Your Partner:

"Are You Married?"

"Do You Have Any Children?"

"How Many Children Do You Have?"

Student Name _____ Date _____

Be the first to ask your partner if they are married or do they have any children. If they have children, ask them how many children they have. After you ask the questions, circle yes or no and have your partner sign this sheet.

I asked my partner if he/she is married?   Yes   No

I asked my partner if he/she has any children?   Yes   No

I asked my partner how many children he/she has? Yes   No

Was the student the first to ask the questions?   Yes   No

Signature: _____

Lesson 39

Be the First to Ask Your Partner:

"Do You Have Any Pets?"

"How Many Pets Do You Have?"

"What Are the Names of Your Pets?"

Student Name _____ Date _____

Be the first to ask your partner if they have any pets. If your partner has pets, ask how many pets they have. Ask what the names of the pets are?

I asked my partner if he/she has any pets?   Yes   No

I asked my partner how many pets he/she has?   Yes   No

I asked my partner the names of her/his pets?   Yes   No

Was the student the first to ask the questions?   Yes   No

Signature: _____

Lesson 40

Be the First to Ask Your Partner:

"How Was Your Weekend?"

"What Did You Do Last Weekend?"

Student Name _____ Date _____

Be the first to ask your partner how they enjoyed the weekend and what they did last weekend. After you ask the questions, circle yes or no and have your partner sign on the line.

I asked my partner: How Was Your Weekend?   Yes   No

I asked my partner: What Did You Do Last Weekend?   Yes   No

Was the student the first to ask the questions?   Yes   No

Signature: _____

Lesson 41

Be the First to Ask Your Partner:

"What Is Your Favorite TV Show?"

"When Do You Watch Your Favorite TV Show?"

Student Name _____ Date _____

Be the first to ask your partner his/her favorite TV show and when do they watch the show? After you ask the questions, circle yes or no and have the person sign on the line.

I asked my partner: What Is Your Favorite TV Show?   Yes   No

Was the student the first to ask the questions?   Yes   No

I asked my partner: When Do You Watch The Show?   Yes   No

Was the student the first to ask the questions?   Yes   No

Signature: _____

Lesson 42

Be the First to Ask Your Partner:

"What Did You Do Last Night?"

"Did You Stay At Home?"

Student Name _____ Date _____

Be the first to ask your partner what he/she did last night. Ask if they stayed at home or went somewhere. After you ask the question, circle yes or no and have the person sign on the line.

I asked my partner: What Did You Do Last Night? Yes   No

I asked my partner: Did You Stay At Home?   Yes   No

Was the student the first to ask the questions?   Yes   No

Signature: _____

Lesson 43

Be the First to Ask Your Partner:

"What Time Do You Go Home Today?"

"What Will You Do When You Get Home?"

Student Name _____ Date _____

Be the first to ask your partner what time he/she goes home today. Ask your partner what he/she will do when they get home. After you ask the questions, circle yes if you were the first to ask the question and no if you were not the first to ask the questions. Have your partner sign on the line.

I asked my partner: What Time Will You Go Home Today?   Yes   No

I asked my partner: What Will You Do When You Get Home? Yes   No

Was the student the first to ask the questions?   Yes   No

Signature: _____

Lesson 44

Be the First to Ask Your Partner:

"How Is Your Day Going?"

"Are You Having A Nice Day?"

Student Name _____ Date _____

Be the first to ask your partner how his/her day is going. Ask if they are having a nice day. After you ask the questions, circle yes or no. Have your partner sign on the line.

I asked my partner: How Is Your Day Going?   Yes   No

I asked my partner: Are You Having A Nice Day? Yes   No

Was the student the first to ask the questions?   Yes   No

Signature: _____

Self-Managed Checklist

Lesson 45

Be the First to Ask Your Partner:

"How Is Your Family?"

"Is Everyone Doing OK?"

Student Name _____ Date _____

Be the first to ask your partner how his/her family is doing. Ask if everyone is doing OK. After you ask the questions, circle yes or no. Have your partner sign on the line.

I asked my partner: How Is Your Family?   Yes   No

I asked my partner: Is Everyone Doing OK?   Yes   No

Was the student the first to ask the questions?   Yes   No

Signature: _____

Lesson 46

Be the First to Ask Your Partner:

"How Are You Today?"

"Are You Feeling OK?"

Student Name _____ Date

Be the first to ask your partner how he/she is doing and if they are feeling OK. When you ask the questions, circle yes or no and have the person write whether you were the first one to ask the questions. Have your partner sign on the line.

I asked my partner: How Are You Doing?   Yes   No

I asked my partner: Are You Feeling OK?   Yes   No

Was the student the first to ask the questions?   Yes   No

Signature: _____

Lesson 47

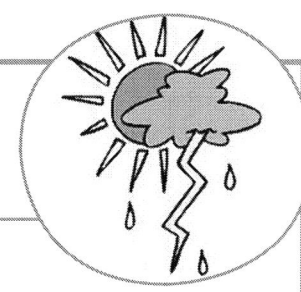

Be the First to Tell Your Partner:

About the Weather Today —
Ask Your Partner How He/She Likes the Weather?

Student Name _____ Date _____

Be the first to talk to your partner about the weather and to ask your partner if he/she likes the weather. When you ask the questions, circle yes or no and have the person write whether you were the first one to ask the questions. Have your partner sign on the line.

I talked to my partner: I Talked About The Weather   Yes   No

I asked my partner: Do You Like The Weather?   Yes   No

Was the student the first to ask the questions?   Yes   No

Signature: _____

Lesson 48

Be the First to:

Smile at Your Partner

Make Eye Contact

Student Name _____ Date _____

Be the first to talk to smile at your partner and to make eye contact with your partner. Have your partner sign on the line.

I was the first to smile at my partner?   Yes No

I was the first to make eye contact with my partner? Yes No

Was the student the first to smile and make eye contact?   Yes   No

Signature _____

Lesson 49

Be the First to:

Shake Your Partner's Hand

Make Eye Contact

Student Name _____ Date _____

Be the first to give your partner a firm handshake and make eye contact.
Have your partner sign on the line.

I was the first to shake my partner's hand?   Yes   No

I was the first to make eye contact with my partner? Yes   No

Was the student the first to shake hands and make eye contact?   Yes   No

Signature_____

Lesson 50

Be the First to:

Give Your Partner a Firm Hand Shake

Make Eye Contact

Smile

Student Name _____ Date _____

Be the first to give your partner a firm handshake, make eye contact and smile. Have your partner sign on the line.

I was the first to give my partner a firm handshake?   Yes No

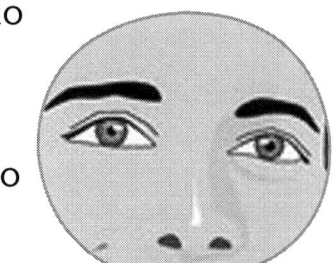

I was the first to make eye contact with my partner?   Yes No

I was the first to smile at my partner?   Yes No

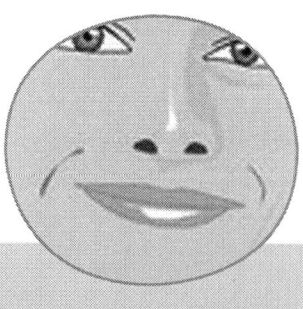

Was the student the first to shake hands, make eye contact, and smile?   Yes   No

Signature_____

Appendix

The following lessons are designed for advanced practice. They can be used after your students have been through the basic training of the **Conversation Skills Program**. These lessons are especially effective after the students have established a rapport with a coworker or a break partner. Students will use the groundwork that has been laid in previous lessons to sharpen and maintain their conversation skills.

Some students will use these lessons as a springboard for their own questions and comments and that is fine.

Lesson 1

"How Long Have You Worked Here?"

"Do You Like Your Work?"

Student Name _____ Date _____

Be the first to ask your coworkers about how long they have worked there and if they like their work. When you ask the question, circle a number and have the person write their names on the line.

1   2   3   4   5

Names of people who told me about their work:

1. _____

2. _____

3. _____

4. _____

5. _____

Supplemental

Lesson 2

"What Is Your Favorite Food?"

"What Is Your Favorite Restaurant?"

Student Name _____ Date _____

Be the first to ask your coworkers and friends about their favorite foods and their favorite restaurants. When you ask the questions, circle a number and have the person write their names on the line.

1   2   3   4   5

Names of people who told me their favorite foods and their favorite restaurants:

1. _____

2. _____

3. _____

4. _____

5. _____

Supplemental

Lesson 3

"Do You Like To Read?"

"What Is Your Favorite Book?"

Student Name _____ Date _____

Be the first to ask your coworkers and friends if they like to read and what their favorite book is. When you ask the questions, circle a number and have them write their names on the line.

1   2   3   4   5

Names of people who told me they like to read and what their favorite book is:

1. _____

2. _____

3. _____

4. _____

5. _____

Supplemental

Lesson 4

"Where Are You From?"

"Where Were You Born?"

Student Name _____ Date _____

Be the first to ask your coworkers and friends where they are from and where they were born. When you ask the questions, circle a number and have them write their names on the line.

1   2   3   4   5

Names of people who told me where they are from and where they were born:

1. _____

2. _____

3. _____

4. _____

5. _____

Supplemental

Lesson 5

"Do You Have A Big Weekend Planned?"

"Will You See Your Family and Friends This Weekend?"

Student Name _____ Date _____

Be the first to ask your coworkers and friends if they have a big weekend planned and if they will see their family and friends. When you ask the questions, circle a number and have them write their names on the line.

1   2   3   4   5

Names of people who told me about their weekend:

1. _____

2. _____

3. _____

4. _____

5. _____

Supplemental

Lesson 6

"What Did You Do Last Weekend?"

"Did You Have Fun?"

Student Name _____ Date _____

Be the first to ask your coworkers and friends where they are from and where they were born. When you ask the questions, circle a number and have them write their names on the line.

1   2   3   4   5

Names of people who told me how their families were:

1. _____

2. _____

3. _____

4. _____

5. _____

Supplemental

Lesson 7

"How Are You Today?"

"Do You Like The Weather?"

Student Name _____ Date _____

Be the first to ask your coworkers and friends how they are doing and how they like the weather. After you ask the questions, circle a number and have the person sign on the line.

1   2   3   4   5

Names of people who told me how they were doing and how they like the weather:

1. _____

2. _____

3. _____

4. _____

5. _____

Supplemental

Lesson 8

"Do You Go To The Movies?"

"What Is Your Favorite Movie?"

Student Name _____ Date _____

Be the first to ask your coworkers and friends if they go to the movies and what their favorite movie is. After you ask the questions, circle a number and have the person sign on the line.

1   2   3   4   5

Names of people who told me they go to the movies and what their favorite movie is:

1. _____

2. _____

3. _____

4. _____

5. _____

Supplemental

Lesson 9

"Do You Have Any Brothers And Sisters?"

"How Many Brothers And Sisters Do You Have?"

Student Name _____ Date _____

Be the first to ask your coworkers and friends if they have any brothers and sisters and how many they have. After you ask the questions, circle a number and have the person sign on the line.

1   2   3   4   5

Names of people who told me about their brothers and sisters:

1. _____

2. _____

3. _____

4. _____

5. _____

Supplemental

Lesson 10

Practice Your Smile And Say Hello

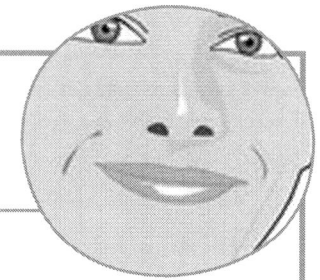

Student Name _____ Date _____

Be the first to smile and say hello to your coworkers and friends. After you smile and say hello, circle a number and have the person sign on the line.

1   2   3   4   5

Names of people whom I told hello and smiled at them:

1. _____

2. _____

3. _____

4. _____

5. _____

Supplemental

Lesson 11

"How Is Your Family?"

"What Are They Doing Today?"

Student Name _____ Date _____

Be the first to ask your coworkers and friends how their family is doing and what their family is doing today. After you ask the questions, circle a number and have the person sign on the line.

1   2   3   4   5

Names of people who told me about their families:

1. _____

2. _____

3. _____

4. _____

5. _____

Supplemental

Lesson 12

"Do You Have Any Children?"

"What Are The Names Of Your Children?"

Student Name _____ Date _____

Be the first to ask your coworkers and friends if they have any children and what the names of their children are. After you ask the questions, circle a number and have the person sign on the line.

1   2   3   4   5

Names of people who told me about their children:

1. _____

2. _____

3. _____

4. _____

5. _____

Supplemental

Lesson 13

"Do You Have Any Pets?"

"What Are The Names Of Your Pets?"

Student Name _____ Date _____

Be the first to ask your coworkers and friends if they have any pets and what the names of their pets are. After you ask the questions, circle a number and have the person sign on the line.

1   2   3   4   5

Names of people who told me about their pets and the names of their pets:

1. _____

2. _____

3. _____

4. _____

5. _____

Supplemental